PROTONS, NEUTRONS, ELECTRONS AND QUARKS!

TINY ATOMS WE CAN'T SEE

SCIENCE FOR KIDS

CHILDREN'S CHEMISTRY BOOKS

pfiffikus

EDUCATIONAL BOOKS FOR CHILDREN K-12

Kids, let's study interesting facts about the three main parts of an atom.

Actually there are five most important subatomic particles. They are the protons, neutrons, electrons, and the positron. These subatomic particles are described by their electrical charge, their mass and their orbit.

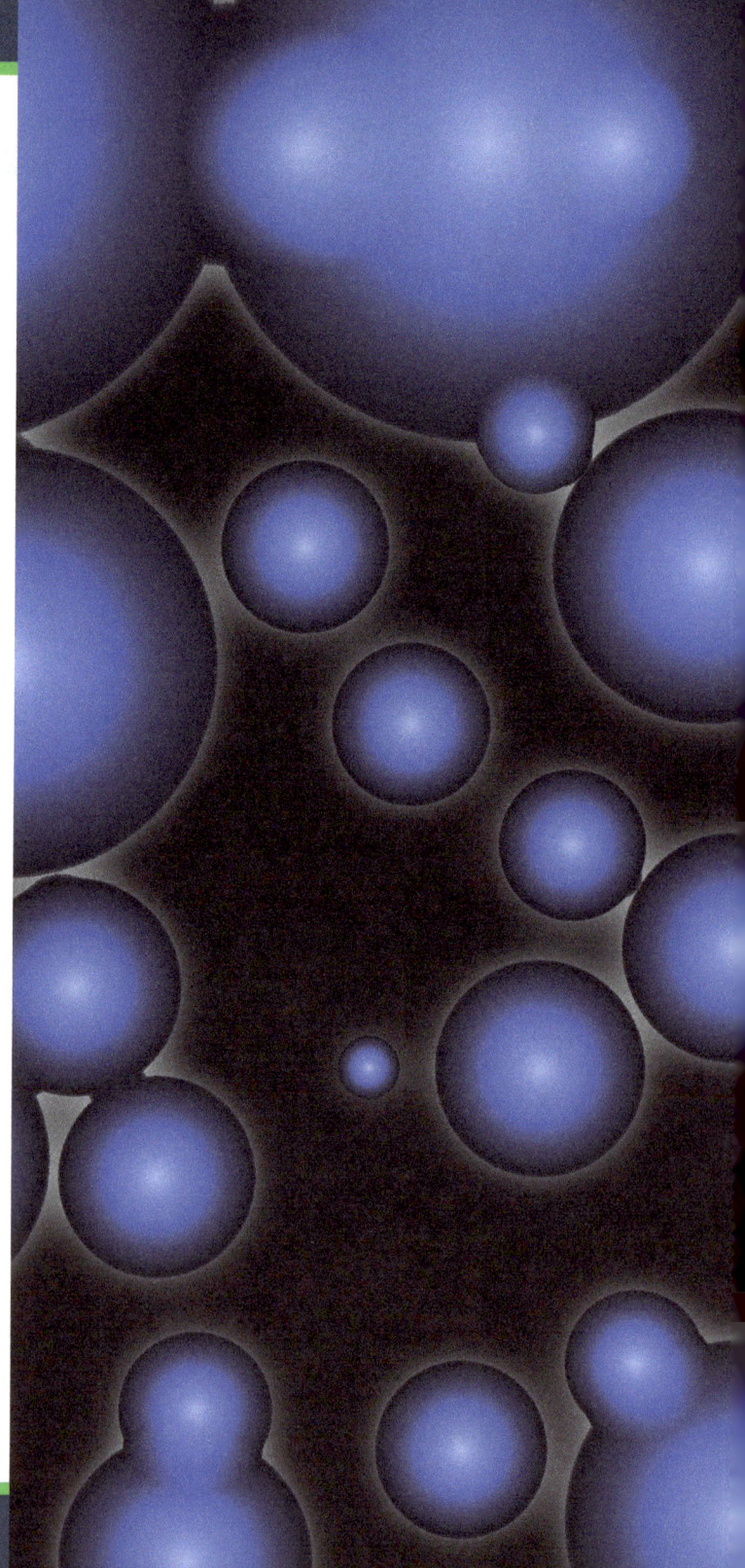

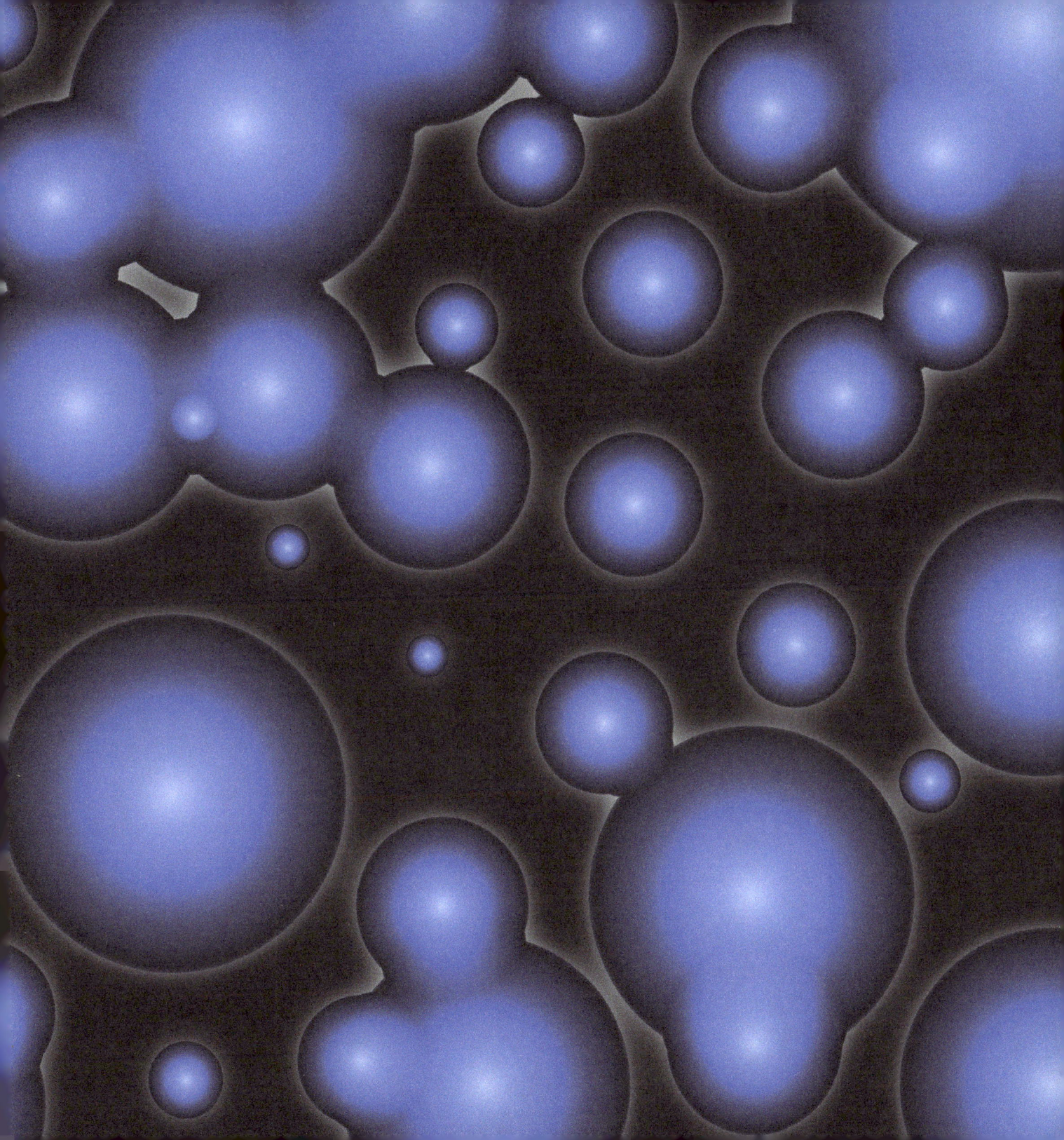

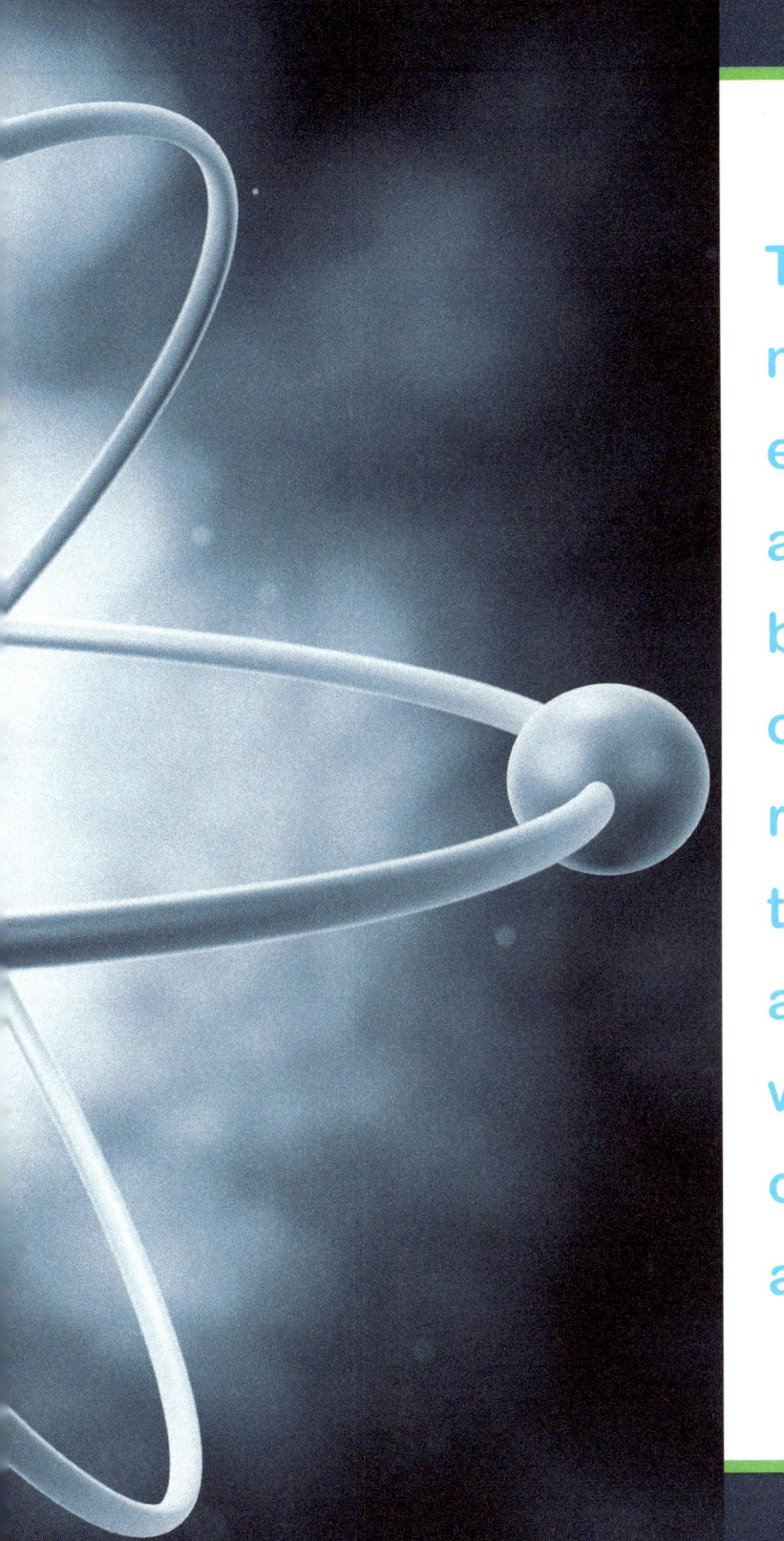

The protons, neutrons and electrons particles are called the building blocks of atom. The remaining two, the neutrons and positrons were discovered outside the Earth's atmosphere.

The nucleus is formed by a clump of protons and neutrons. They are at the center of the atom. Protons possess positive electrical charge while the neutrons have no electrical charge.

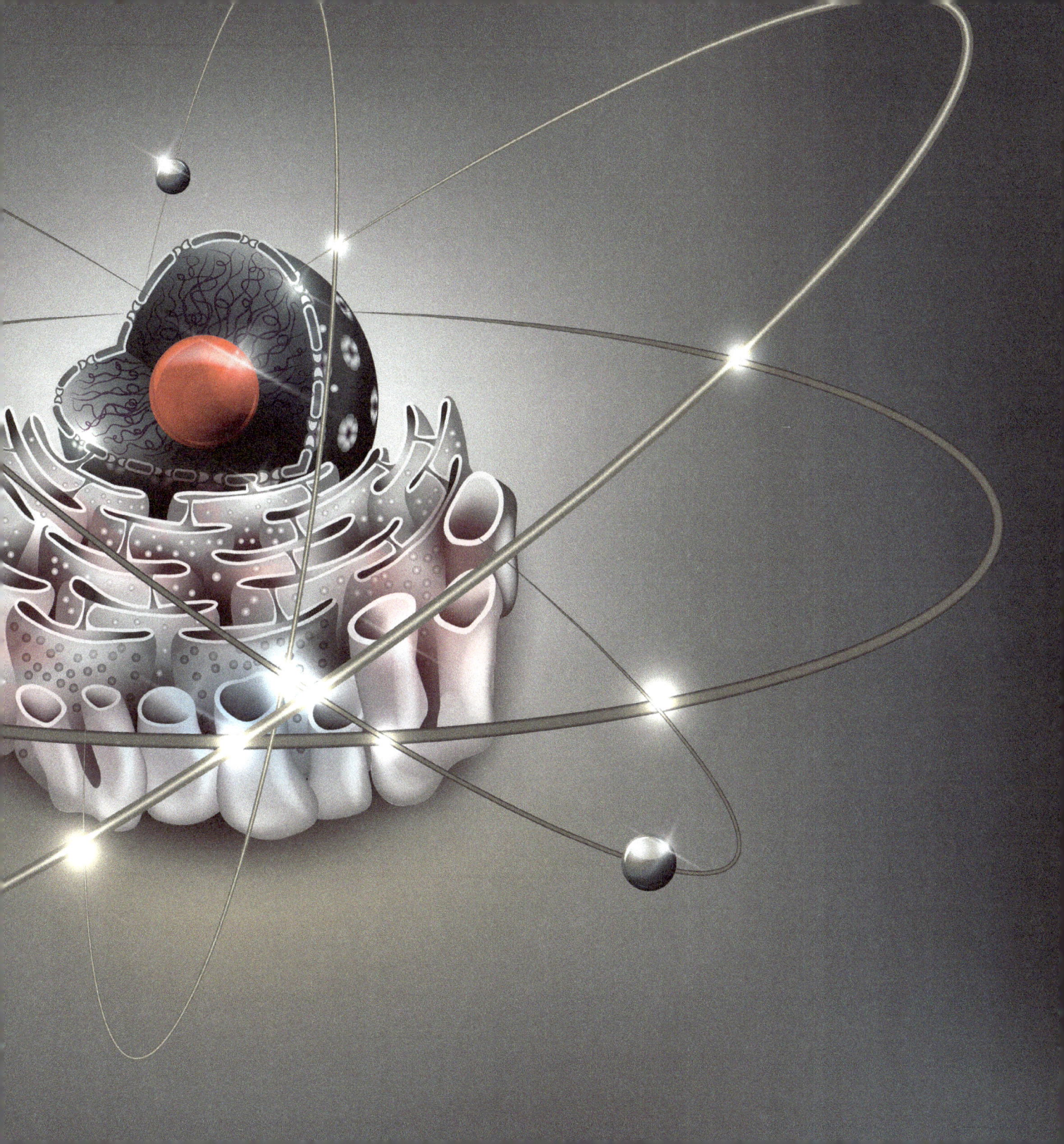

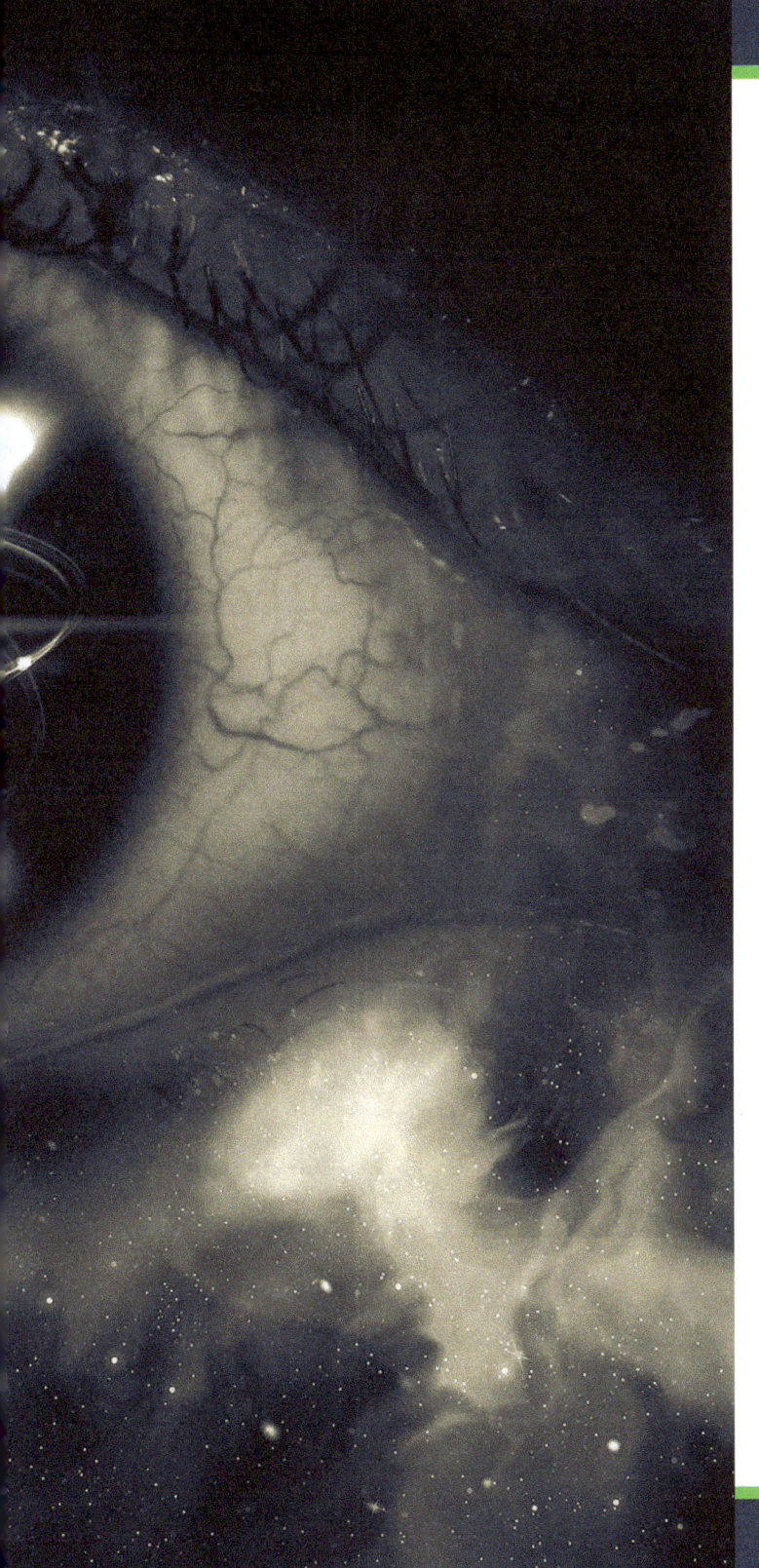

The electrons are outside the nucleus. They orbit rapidly around the nucleus. The electrons hold a negative electrical charge. This is to balance the positively charged protons.

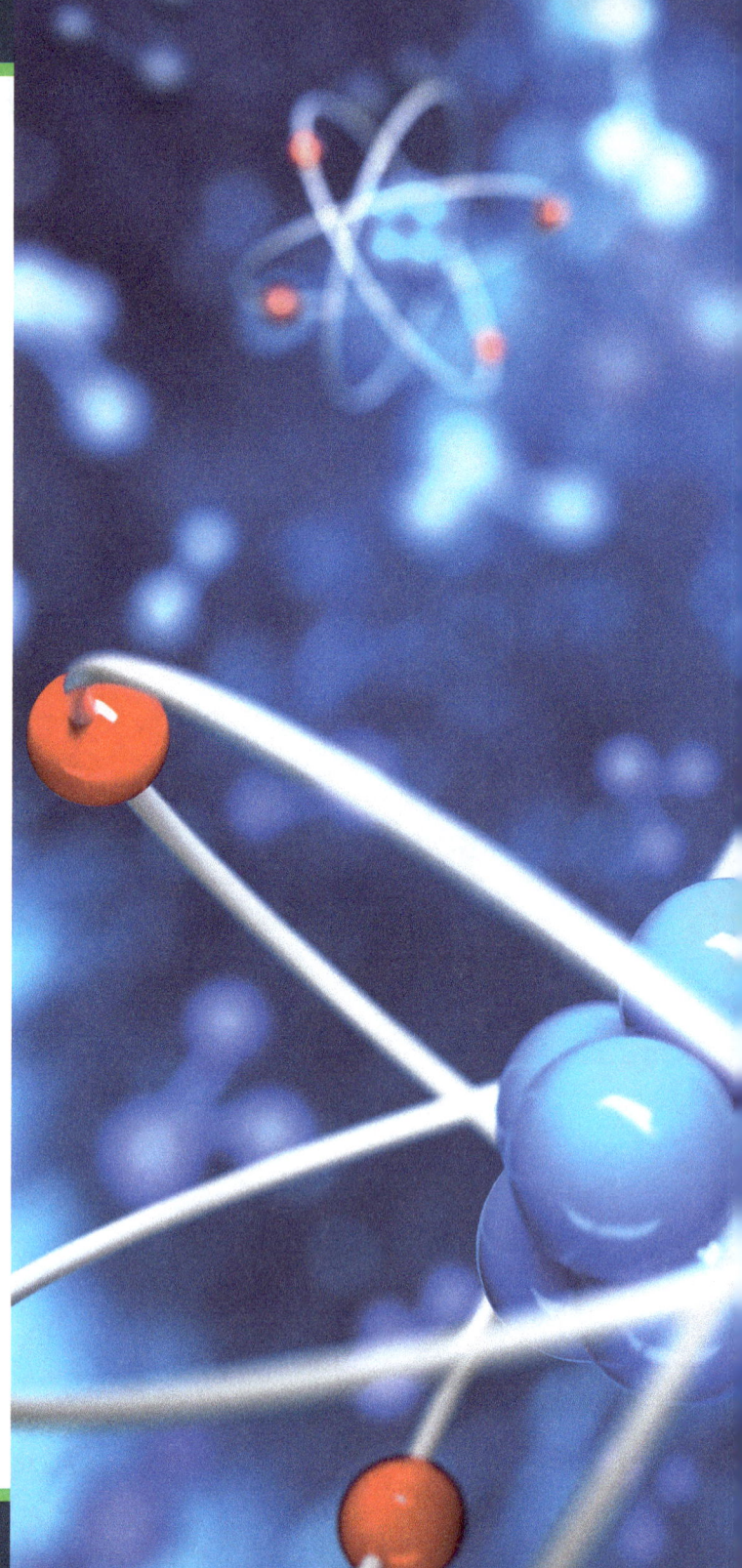

Elements are made up of smallest particles called atoms. A different number of protons made up each element. Atoms are very small.

They can't be seen. Yet, they are studied as to how they behave. Interestingly, protons and neutrons are parallel in mass while electrons have less mass for they are smaller.

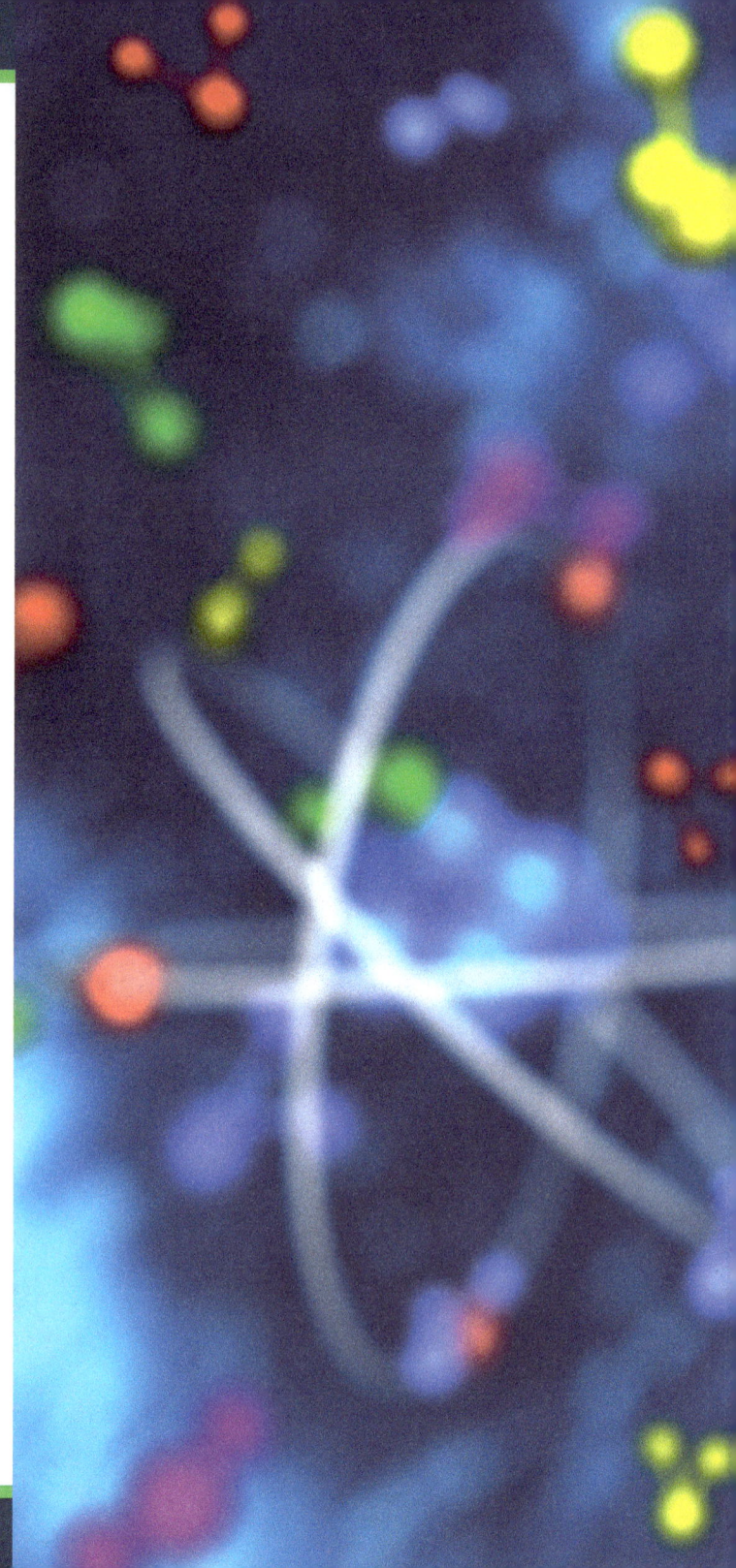

These subatomic particles move all the time. The movement of the electrons outside the nucleus prevents it from bumping into it. They hold the atom together.

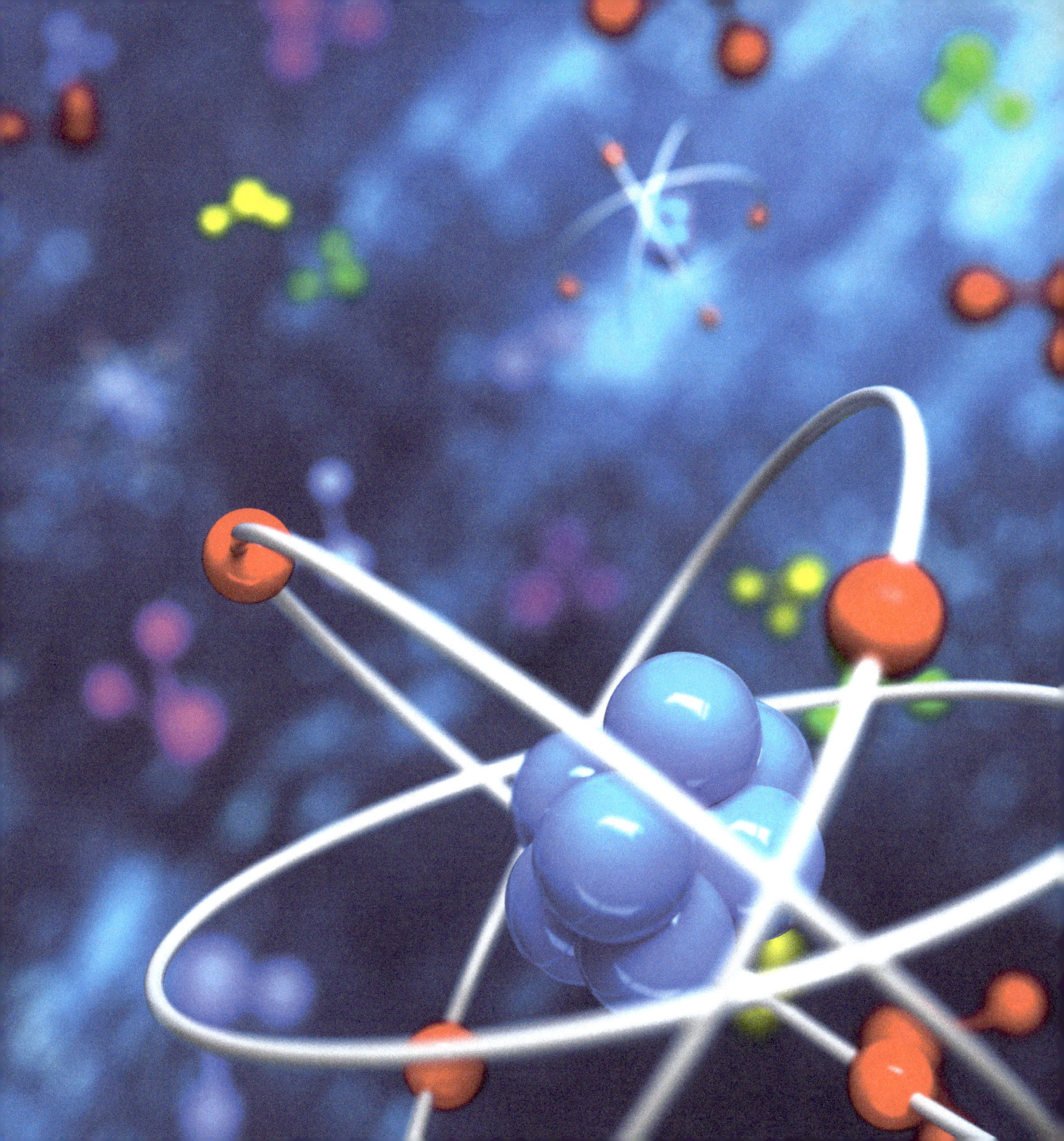

Electrons follow different orbits. They are in layers known as shells. They resemble a cloud floating quickly around the nucleus. Because electrons move at very high speed, their location is hard to pin down.

A proton has an atomic mass of 1 amu. They are considered as one of the important compositions of an atom.

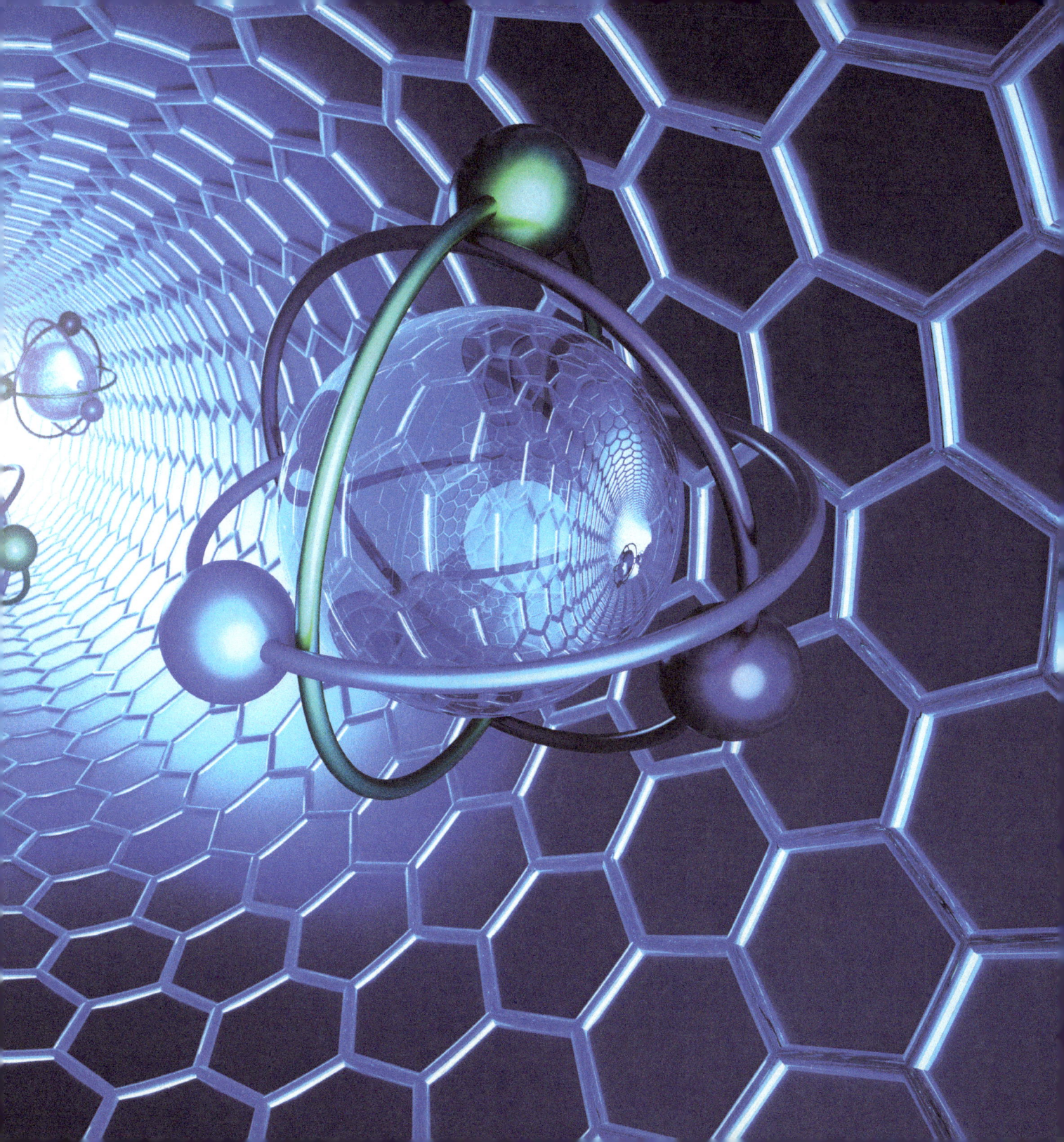

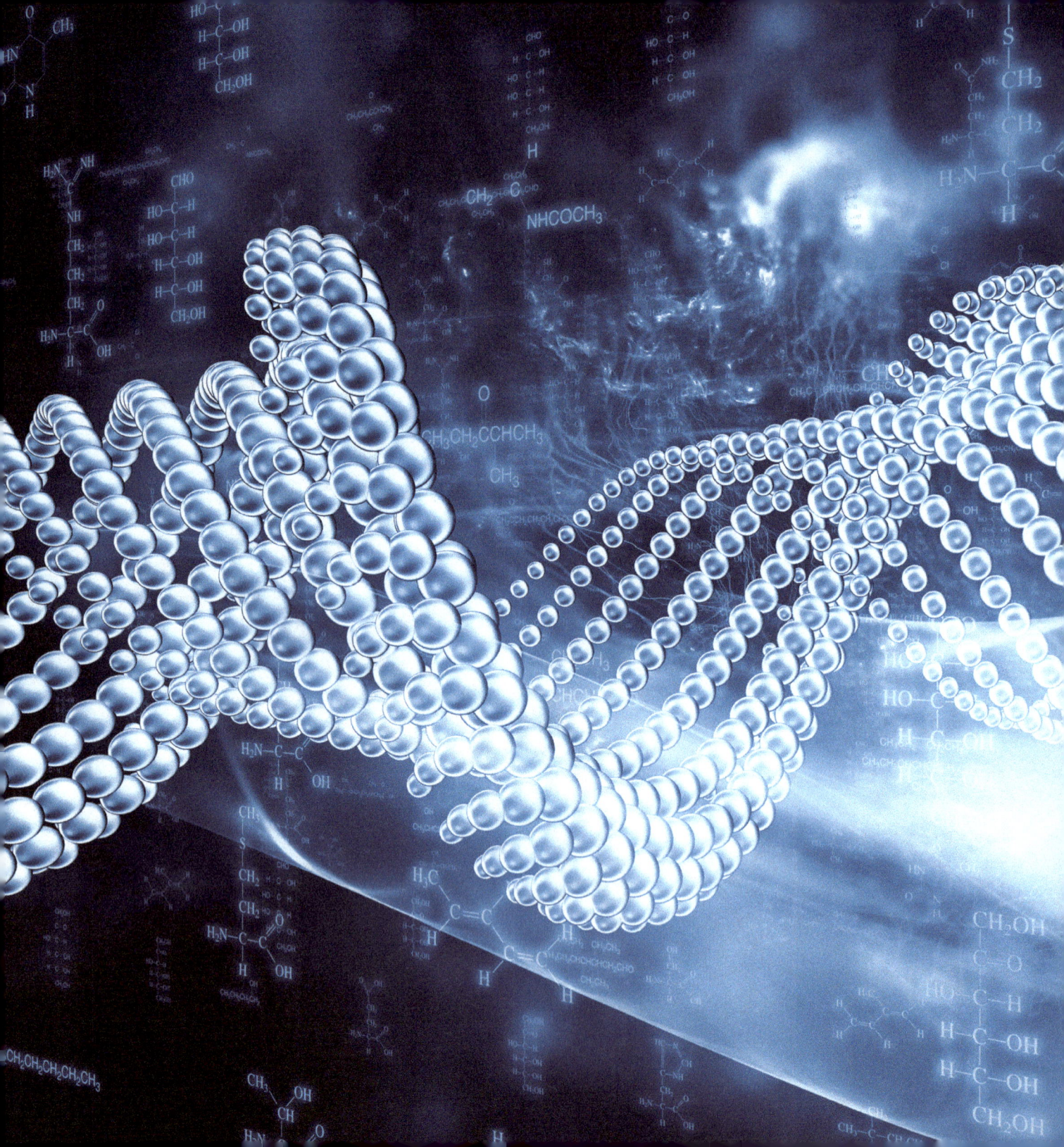

The chemical identity of an atom is determined by the number of protons.

This identity is the atomic number. The number of protons an atom contains gives its atomic number. The number of proton and neutrons inside an atom determines the atomic mass or atomic weight.

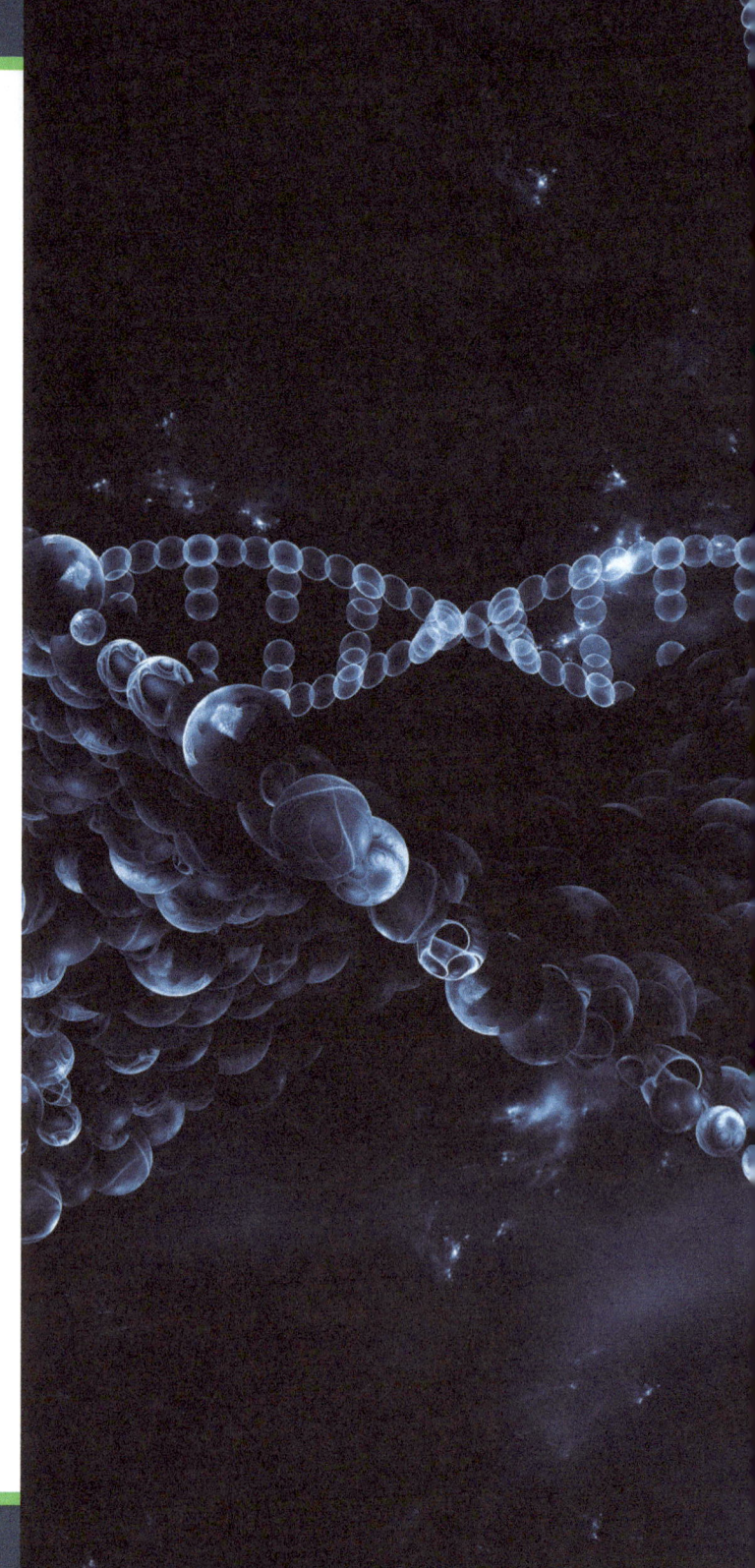

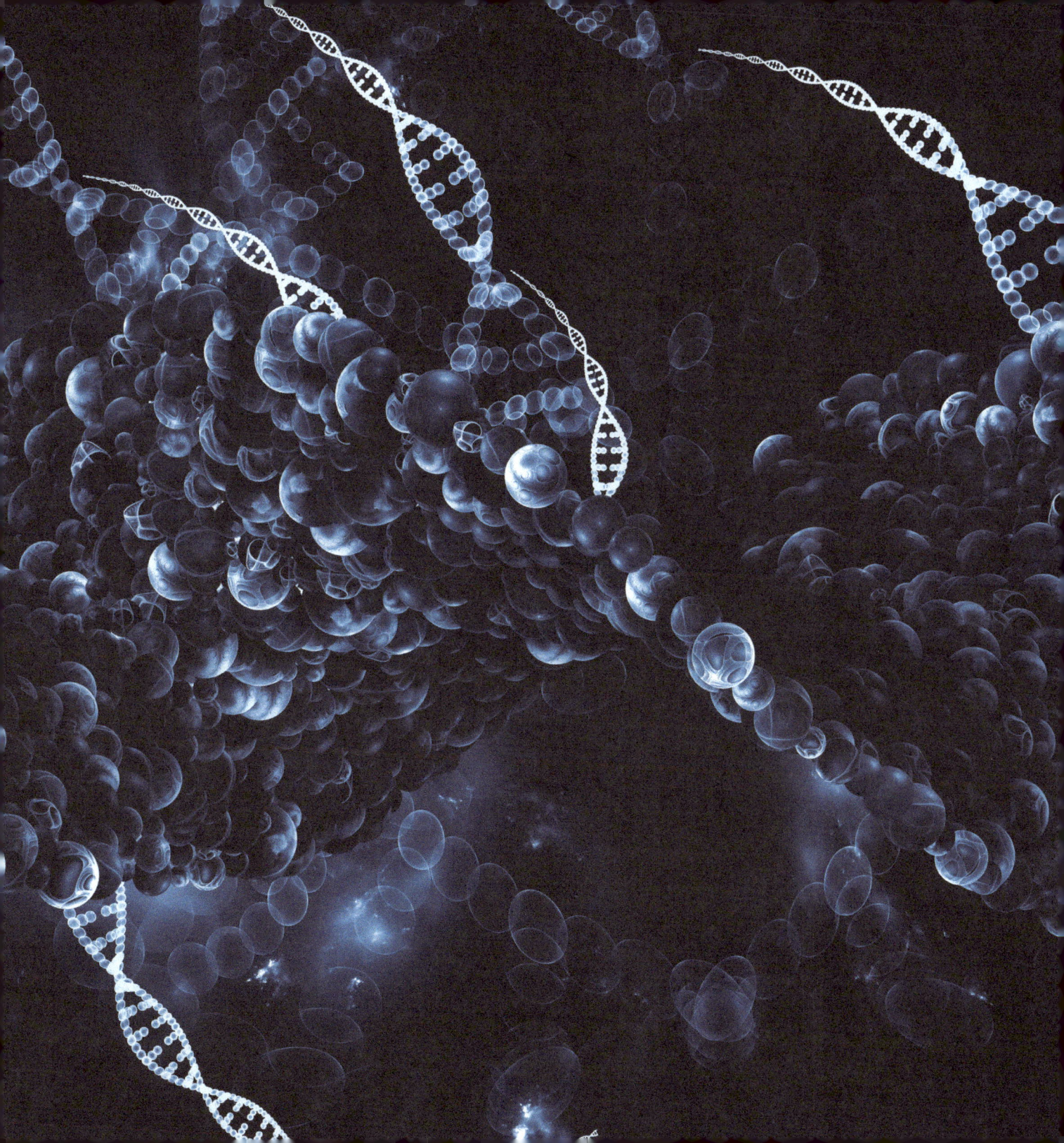

A neutron weighs 1 amu. It holds no electrical charge. It is found along with the protons in the nucleus of atoms. Neutrons are considered as stable particles.

They stay the same for an infinite period of time. The elements which are composed of the same number of protons but different number of neutrons are known as isotopes.

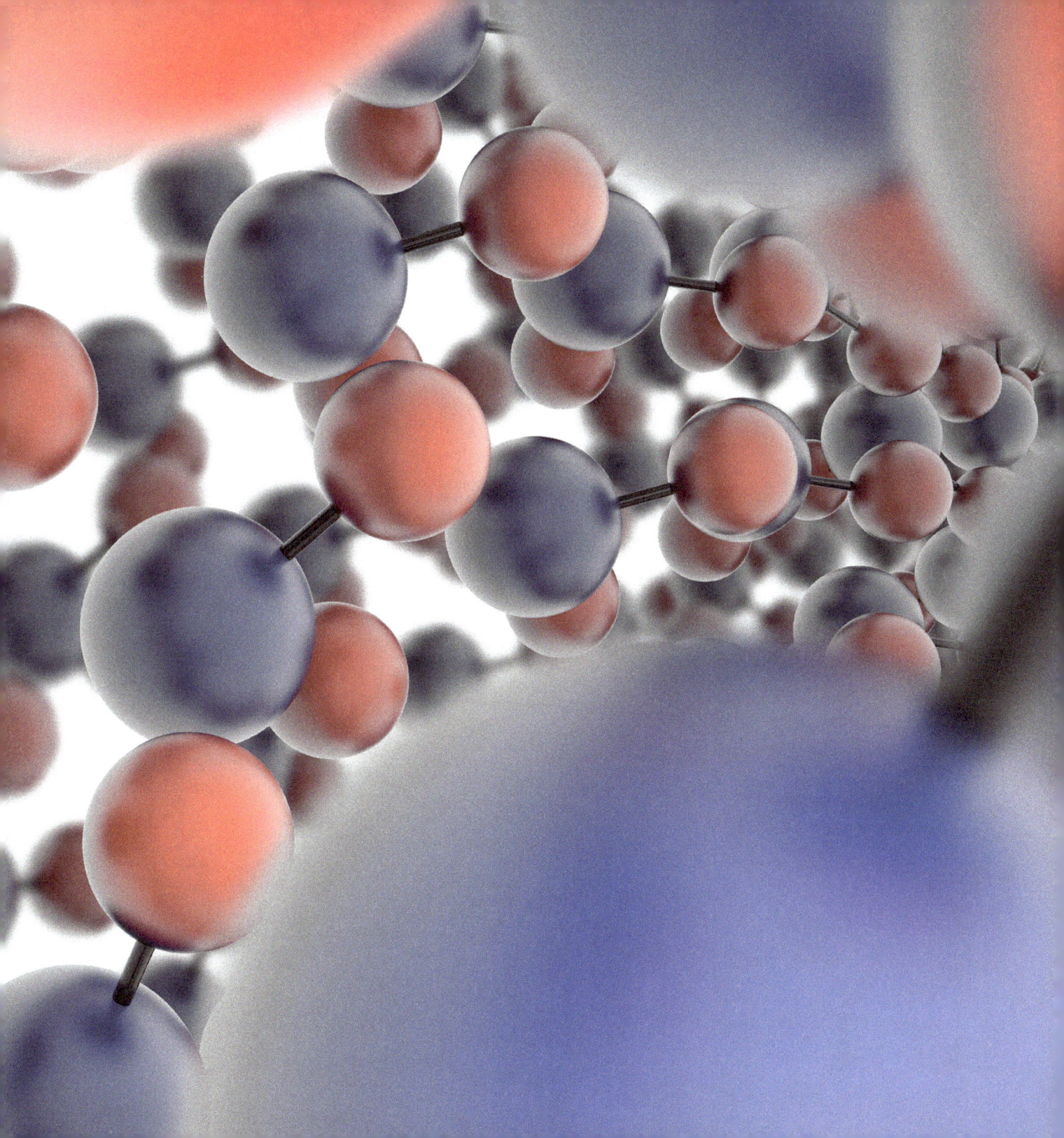

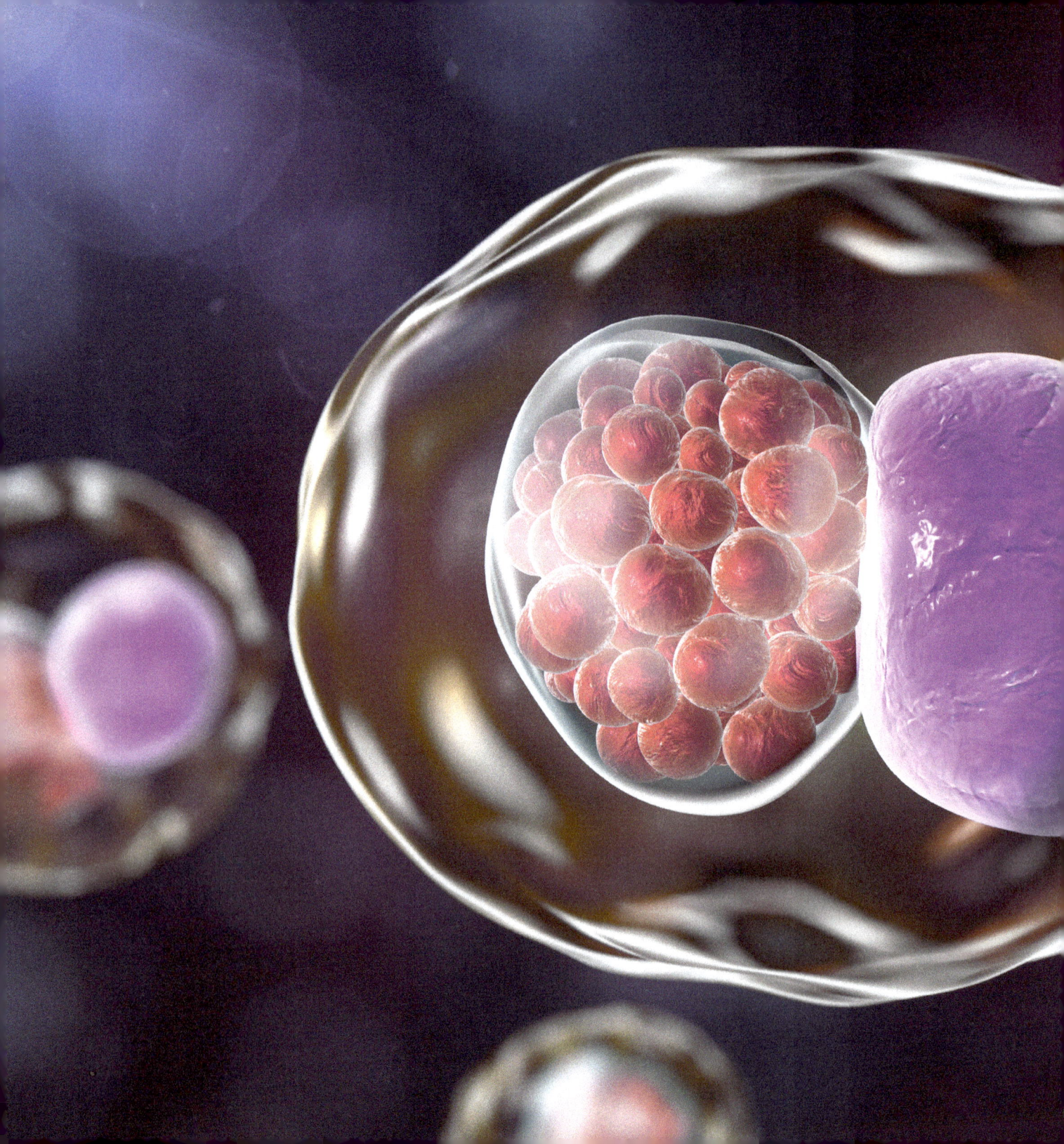

They are found outside the nucleus. They are negatively charged. Electrons are elementary particles. They can't be broken down.

The two main categories of elementary particles are the fermions and bosons. Fermions are the particles in matter which are divided into two types of particles. These are the quarks and the leptons.

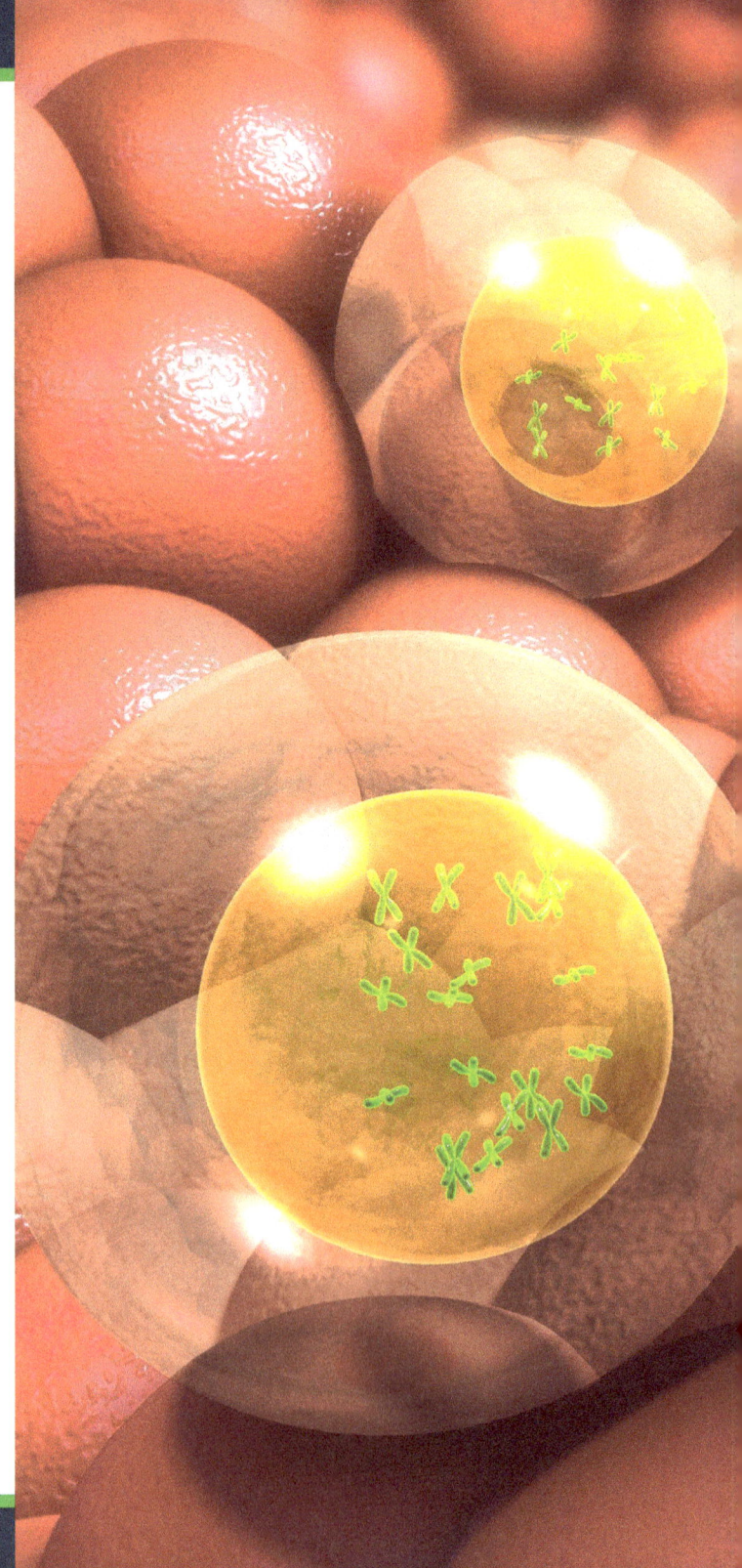

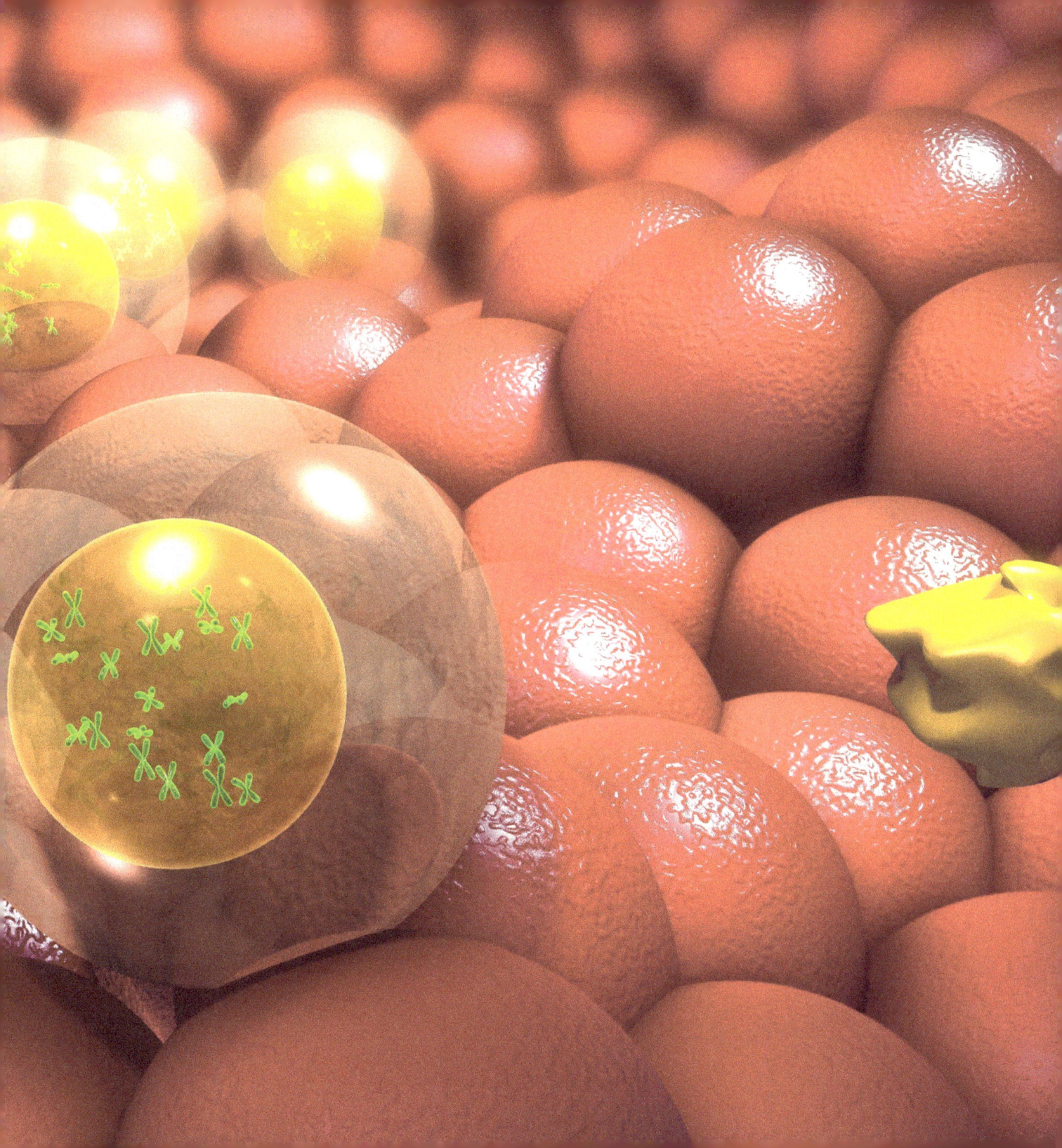

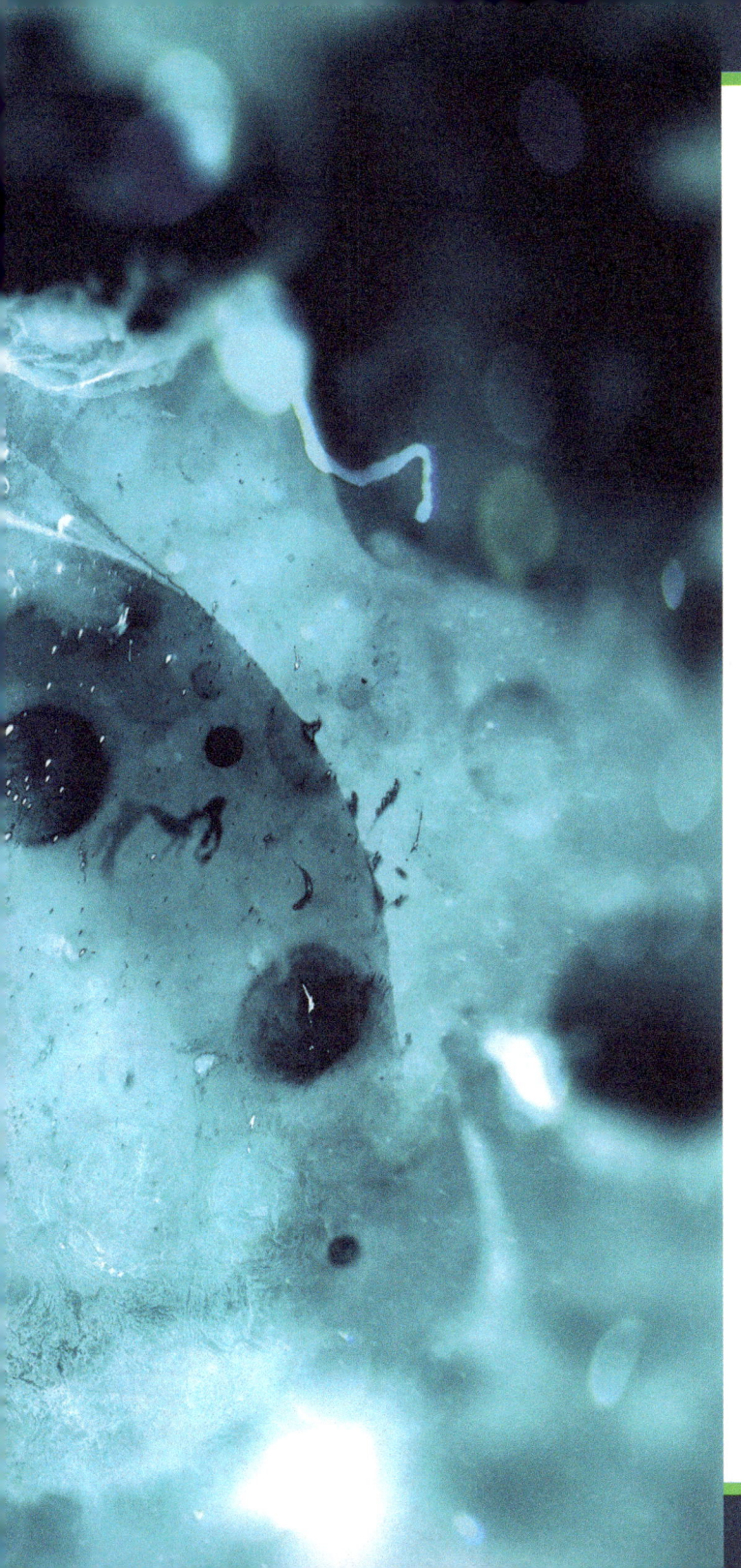

Protons and neutrons have basic building blocks known as the quarks. Quarks come in six types with their interesting names. Examples are charm, up, down top and bottom.

On the other hand, electrons are considered leptons and are important building blocks of atoms. This breakdown of atomic particles made us understand that atoms are very small, yet they are composed of subatomic particles.

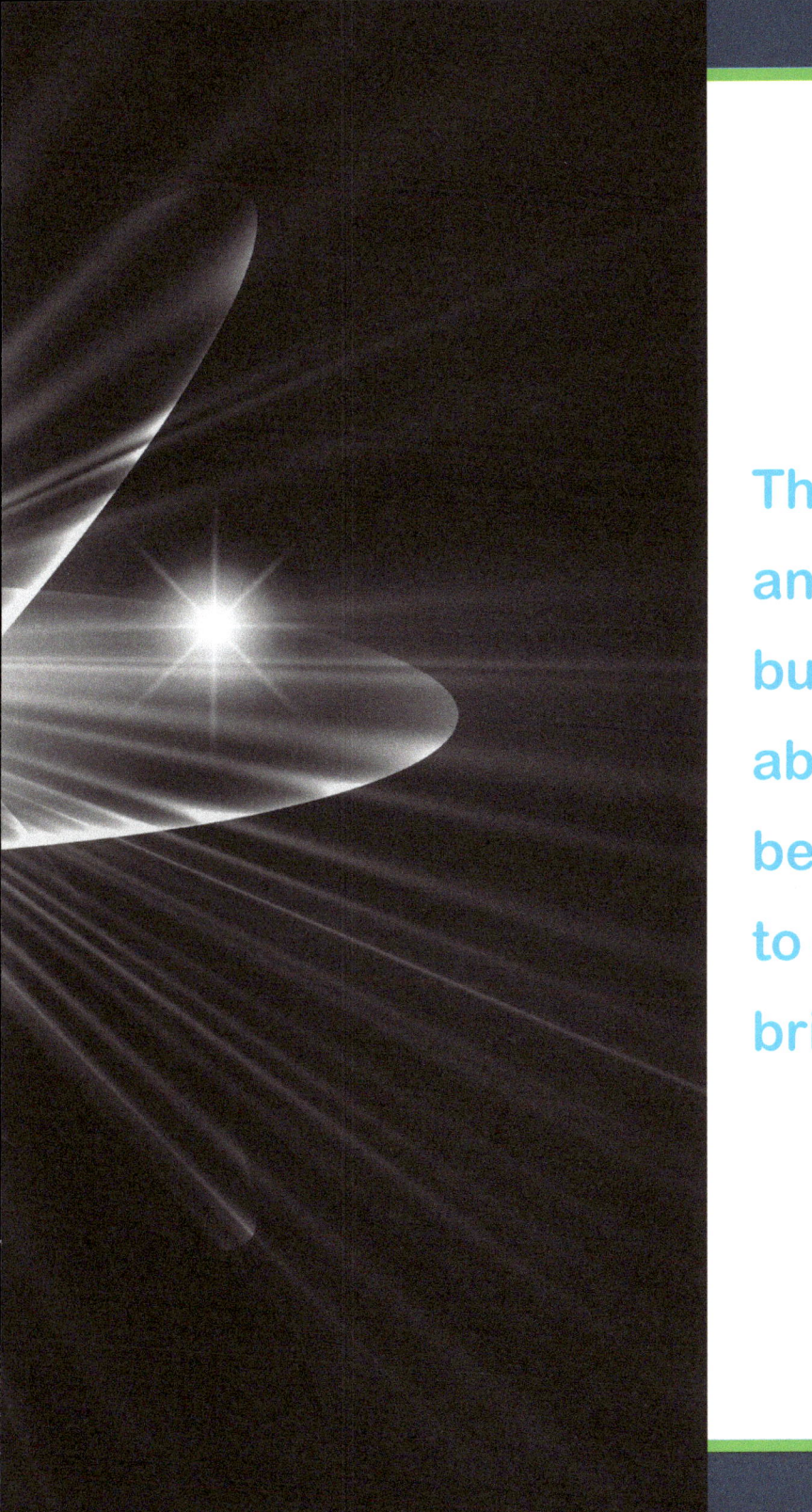

They are very small and can't be seen but people were able to study their behaviour. Thanks to our patient and brilliant scientists.